BIOGRAPHY

150 Facts You Won't Believe!

HUGH WESTRUP

Cover and interior illustrations
by Robert Roper

SCHOLASTIC INC.
New York Toronto London Auckland Sydney
Mexico City New Delhi Hong Kong

ISBN 0-439-16366-8

Text copyright © 2000 by Scholastic Inc. Illustrations copyright © 2000 by Scholastic Inc.
All rights reserved. Published by Scholastic Inc.

SCHOLASTIC and associated logos are trademarks and/or registered trademarks of Scholastic Inc.

12 11 10 9 8 7 6 5 4 3 2   0 1 2 3 4 5/0

Printed in the U.S.A.   01

First Scholastic printing, January 2000

TABLE OF CONTENTS

- The great German composer Johann Sebastian Bach (1685–1750) had 76 male relatives. Most of them were musicians and 53 of them were named Johann.

- Oscar-winning actress Mary Pickford (1893–1979) became "America's Sweetheart" playing young girls in the movies. To make Pickford look small, the sets and props in her movies were built larger than normal.

- Bugs Bunny (1939–) was named after Ben "Bugs" Hardaway, a writer and director of Hollywood cartoons.

- Actress May Irwin (1862–1938) puckered up with actor James Rice for the first big-screen smooch in *The Fifty-Foot Kiss* (1896). The kiss angered preachers and newspapermen, but Irwin went on to even greater fame and fortune as a dancer, singer, writer, and funny lady.

- Samuel Taylor Coleridge (1772–1834) was a well-known English critic and poet, whose verses include *The Rime of the Ancient Mariner* and *Kubla Khan*. Samuel Coleridge-Taylor (1875–1912) was also a famous Englishman. He was the first black man to achieve fame as a musical composer.

- Igor Stravinsky (1882–1971) was a leading composer of classical music in the 20th century. His famous works for the ballet include *The Firebird* and *The Rite of Spring*. He also wrote a piece called *Do Not Throw Paper Towels in the Toilet*.

NEW STRAVINSKY BALLET

DO NOT THROW **PAPER TOWELS** IN THE TOILET

A BEAUTIFUL MELDING OF DANCE AND WASTE WATER!

- Lorenzo Da Ponte (1749–1838) wrote the words for three of Wolfgang Amadeus Mozart's operas, *Così fan tutte, Don Giovanni,* and *The Marriage of Figaro.* In 1808, Da Ponte moved from Europe to Philadelphia, Pennsylvania, and opened a grocery store.

- As a young man, the comedian W.C. Fields (1880–1946) worked as a professional "drowner" at a seaside theater.

Fields pretended to be drowning in the ocean and the commotion would attract people nearby. After Fields was "saved," the bystanders were encouraged to step into the theater and see the show.

- John Howard Payne (1791–1852) composed the well-known song "Home Sweet Home." Payne lived most of his life on the road and died homeless in a foreign country.

- Fred Waring (1900–1984) led a popular Big Band in the 1930s and composed some 200 songs. He also financed the development and marketing of the popular food processor, the Waring Blender.

- Johann Strauss (1825–1899) and his touring orchestra were as popular in the 19th century as any rock or rap group is today. Like rock and rap, the waltz wasn't approved by everyone. One doctor said that too much waltzing could drive people insane.

- In 1942, Hedy Lamarr (1913–1959) and a Hollywood composer, George Antheil (1900–1959), came up with an idea that, years later, became the basis for today's cellular telephones.

- Irving Berlin (1888–1989), America's greatest composer of popular songs, never learned to read or write music. The composer of "White Christmas" and "God Bless America" merely hummed or sang his songs to a secretary, who took them down in proper musical form.

- Mollie Bailey (1841–1918) of Mobile, Alabama, eloped as a teenager with James Bailey, a circus musician. Mollie's parents disapproved of the circus so much that they disowned Mollie. But the lure of the big top was so strong for Mollie that she went on to become the only woman in history to own and operate her own circus, The Mollie Bailey Show.

- Actress Hattie McDaniel (1895–1952) was not invited to the world premiere of *Gone With the Wind* (1939) in Atlanta, Georgia. The idea of an African-American attending such a high-profile event was considered too upsetting in the racially segregated South. Nevertheless, McDaniel went on to receive an Academy Award for her performance as Mammy in *GWTW* and became the first African-American to win an Oscar.

- Frank Sinatra (1915–1998) became a singing superstar in the early 1940s. When it snowed, his fans would carefully shovel out his footprints, take them home, and store them in their fridges.

- Lena Gilbert Ford (?–1918) wrote the lyrics to the popular song "Keep the Home Fires Burning." She burned to death in 1918 when her home caught fire.

- John Wayne (1907–1979), America's most popular star of Hollywood westerns, was not fond of horses.

- The oldest recorded personal name in history belonged to a king who lived about 5,000 years ago in Egypt. His name was Sekhen.

- To make sure that her son Nero (37–68) became emperor of Rome, Nero's mother, Agrippina the Younger (15?–59), poisoned the reigning emperor, Claudius, who was her husband. Several years later, Nero had Agrippina executed.

- Inés de Castro was a Spanish woman who fell in love with Pedro, the son of Afonso IV, king of Portugal. The king hated that his son was in love with Inés and had her murdered in 1355. Several years later, when King Afonso died and Pedro became king, Inés's rotting body was unearthed and propped up on the queen's throne.

- After a fight with the Australian government in 1970, farmer Leonard Casley declared his land a separate country — Hutt

River Province. He pronounced himself Prince Leonard and his wife Princess Shirley and made stamps, money, a flag, and a national anthem for his new country. Instead of taking Casley to court, the Australian government has simply ignored him.

- Catherine de' Medici (1519–1589), a queen of France during the 16th century, was an expert on poisons. She delivered secretly poisoned food to poor people and then observed their reactions when they got sick.

- Phiops II (ca. 2294–2200 B.C.), a pharaoh in ancient Egypt, ruled longer than any other monarch in history. He took power at age six and died 94 years later.

- Abdul Kassem Ismael (938–995), a Persian ruler in the 10th century, never traveled anywhere without his library of 117,000 books. The volumes were carried by a caravan of 400 camels trained to walk in alphabetical order.

- Before he became king of France, Louis Philippe (1773–1850) lived abroad for 20 years. Three of those years he spent living in a room over a bar in Philadelphia.

- Eleanor of Aquitaine (1122?–1204) was the wife of King Louis VII of France and later of King Henry II of England. She presided over the Court of Love. People brought their love troubles before the court, and Eleanor and a jury of great ladies dispensed advice to the lovelorn.

- The character of Dracula is based on a real person, Vlad Tepes (1431–1477), a medieval prince of Wallachia (now part of Romania). Vlad, who was also called Vlad the Impaler and Dracula, was not a vampire. He was unbelievably cruel, though, and tortured and murdered thousands of his own people.

- Five hundred years after Dracula, the murderous, thieving dictator Nicolae Ceauşescu (1918–1989) ruled modern-day Romania. Ceauşescu had Vlad Tepes made a national hero and in 1976 put Vlad's image on a stamp.

- Queen Victoria of England (1819–1901) grew up at a time when women were not allowed to have drugs while giving birth. The men who controlled the Church thought childbirth was meant to be painful. Victoria demanded drugs, however, and the Church ceased its objections to the practice from then on.

- Alfred the Great (849–899) of England became a hero to his people for turning back a rising tide of Viking invaders. Alfred believed that he was descended from Adam, Noah, and Methusaleh in the Bible and from Woden, the chief Norse god.

- Victoria Woodhull (1838–1927) was the first woman to run for president of the United States. In 1872, she was the candidate for the Equal Rights Party. During the last four years of her life, Woodhull feared she would die if she went to bed, so she did all her sleeping sitting in a chair.

- Queen Elizabeth I (1533–1603) ruled England in the days before plumbing. She scheduled her progress from one castle to another by leaving whenever the stench from human waste became too much for her to bear.

- King Louis XIV of France (1638–1715) took only three baths during his lifetime.

- Robert E. Lee (1807–1870) was offered command of the army from both sides in the American Civil War. Though he opposed slavery and did not think the South could win, he chose to command the Southern forces because his home state was Virginia.

- Empress Elizabeth Petrovna of Russia (1709–1762) was one of history's greatest clotheshorses. She owned 15,000 dresses and changed outfits two or even three times in an evening.

- Czar Paul I of Russia (1754–1801) got so angry when people made jokes about his being bald that he issued a decree stating anyone who mentioned his baldness in his presence would be sentenced to death.

- Civil rights leader Martin Luther King Jr. (1929–1968) was named Michael Luther King Jr. when he was born, after his father, Michael Luther King Sr. Five years later, for unexplained reasons, King Sr. changed his first name and his son's first name to Martin. Even after that, father and son were never called Martin by their friends but simply "Big Mike" and "Little Mike" or "Daddy King" and "M.L."

- James Jesse Strang (1813–1856) was a Mormon elder who broke away from the church and established a tiny kingdom with several hundred followers on Beaver Island in Lake Michigan. Dressed in a flowing robe and a metal crown, Strang assumed the title of James I, King of Zion. The king was good to his subjects in many ways, but his downfall came when he ordered the women to wear short skirts over long, loose trousers. Two angry husbands who did not like the sight of their wives in pants killed the first and last King of Zion.

- Theagenes, a boxer who lived in ancient Greece, has been called the greatest killer in sports history. In the ancient world, boxers pummeled each other until one or the other — or both — dropped dead. Theagenes won more than 1,400 of those brutal matches.

- Heavyweight boxing champ Gene Tunney (1898–1978) lectured on William Shakespeare at Yale University.

- In 1926, Gertrude Ederle (1906–) became the first woman to swim the English Channel. She swam it two hours faster than the fastest man and her record stood until 1964, when it was broken by another woman, Denmark's Greta Andersen.

- On July 2, 1994, Edward Royds-Jones of England became the oldest man ever to parachute. He was 95 years and 170 days old.

- The six Sutter brothers from Canada have been called "the most remarkable family in the history of American sport." Brian, Darryl, Duane, Brent, Rich, and Ron Sutter all played for the National Hockey League as adults. In 1986, all six Sutters made it into the NHL playoffs.

- Achillia was a female gladiator who fought in ancient Roman amphitheaters. Her bout with another gal gladiator, Amazonia, is depicted in a carving that is now on view in a London museum.

- Mildred "Babe" Didrikson Zaharias (1914–1956) is considered by many to have been the best all-around athlete of the 20th century. Babe excelled at golf, track and field, basketball, baseball, swimming, tennis, and bowling.

- Tennis champion Eleanor Sears (1881–1968) made headlines when she dared to roll up her sleeves and expose her bare arms to the public.

- Scott Statler was just four years old in 1962 when he became the youngest person ever to score a hole in one. He did it on his dad's golf course in Greensburg, Pennsylvania.

- Jackie Mitchell (1914–1987) was the first woman to play professional baseball. Mitchell was the pitcher for Chattanooga, Tennessee, in an exhibition game against the New York Yankees. She pitched against two legendary players, Lou Gehrig and Babe Ruth, and struck out both of them!

- Chung Kwun Ying from Hong Kong was just eight years old in 1986 when he did 2,750 handstand push-ups in a row and broke the world's record.

- Louis Cyr (1863–1912) was a French-Canadian mountain of muscle who was proclaimed in 1896 "the strongest man in the world." At the height of his powers, Cyr lifted 551 pounds with the middle finger of one hand and back-lifted a platform holding 18 men weighing a total of 4,337 pounds.

- The longest shot ever made in pro basketball was thrown on November 13, 1967, by Jerry Harkness of the Indiana Pacers. A regulation basketball court is 94 feet long. Harkness's last-second shot, which won the game for the Pacers, covered 92 feet!

- Byron "Whizzer" White (1917–) was a superb athlete who played for three years in the National Football League. He quit to pursue a career in law and was appointed to the U.S. Supreme Court in 1962.

- Cassius Clay's (1942–) career almost ended before it got off the ground. As a teenager, Clay was diagnosed with a heart murmur and told to stop boxing. Fortunately, the murmur disappeared and Clay went on to become "The Greatest" — Muhammad Ali.

- Jean-François Gravelet (1824–1897) was a French acrobat known as "Blondin" who became famous for walking a tightrope strung high above Niagara Falls on numerous occasions. One time, he crossed the falls blindfolded. On another, he carried his terrified business manager on his back. Blondin's most bizarre crossing had him carrying a small stove halfway across, then cooking and eating an omelette there.

- Mary, Queen of Scots (1542–1587), was probably the first woman golfer. Raised in France, Mary called her royal assistants by the French title *cadets*. On the golf course, the *cadets* carried Mary's golf clubs. Hence, the origin of the word *caddie*.

- In 1911, Calbraith Rodgers (1879–1912) became the first person to fly an airplane across the United States. The plane crashed many times along the way and had to be constantly rebuilt. By the time he reached California, 50 days after taking off from New York, only two of the plane's original parts — the rudder and the oil pan — had made the entire journey.

- Nellie Bly (1867–1922) was the most famous journalist of her day. Her greatest feat was when she beat the fictional record of Jules Verne's *Around the World in Eighty Days*. Traveling by steamship, ricksha, train, and sampan, Bly made the trip in 72 days, 6 hours, and 11 minutes.

- Charles Waterton (1782–1865) was a British naturalist and writer who thrilled readers with stories of his encounters with wild animals. Among other things, Waterton wrestled a boa constrictor, kissed an orangutan, rode a 10-foot alligator, and tried to get a vampire bat to suck blood from his big toe.

- Jeannette Picard (1895–1981) was terrified of heights. Nevertheless, in 1934, she became the first woman in history to go into space — in a balloon that rose to an altitude of 57,579 feet. Forty years later, Picard and 10 other women became the first ordained women priests of the Episcopal Church.

- One of the great mysteries of mountaineering involves George Mallory (1886–1924), a British schoolteacher. Twenty-nine years before Edmund Hillary and Tenzing Norgay conquered Mount Everest in 1953, Mallory and university student Andrew Irvine attempted the climb. Their bodies were recently found on the mountain, but whether they reached the summit is unknown.

- Mary Kingsley (1862–1900) was a British explorer of West Africa who was almost killed when she accidentally fell into a pit that had sharp wooden spikes at the bottom. The pit was a trap made by the Fang, a tribe of cannibals. The Fang did not eat Kingsley, however, and she spent time living with them and studying their customs.

- Catalina de Erauso (1585–1650) was a Spanish nun who ran away from her convent and lived as a man. Tall and muscular, de Erauso made her way to South America, where she gambled, dueled, and frequently got into trouble with the law. During one nighttime duel, she did not realize that her opponent was her own brother and killed him.

- Annie Edison Taylor was 63 years old in 1901 when she became the first person to ride over Niagara Falls in a barrel. "It was a terrible nightmare," she said later.

- Frances Slocum (1773–1847) was five years old when Indians abducted her from her home in Pennsylvania in 1778. Her family did not find her for more than 50 years. By then, she had married a warrior chief, taken the name Maconaqua (Little Bear), raised several children, and completely forgotten how to speak English.

- Martín Pinzón (ca. 1441–1493) was the commander of the *Pinta*, one of the three ships that sailed on Christopher Columbus's historic expedition. It was Pinzón who suggested the change in course that steered the ships in the direction of the island of San Salvador, where the explorers made their first landing on October 12, 1492.

- Before her airplane got lost in the Pacific Ocean, Amelia Earhart (1897–1937) led an extraordinary life. She was not just a pilot but a teacher, a social worker, a lecturer — and a clothing designer. Earhart designed dresses, belts, shirts, blouses, coats, and hats, and her line of clothes was sold in department stores across the country.

- George Washington (1732–1799) had several sets of false teeth. They were made from lead, elephant tusks, and cow, hippopotamus, and human teeth.

- The latter half of President John Adams's (1735–1826) administration was known as the Federalist Reign of Terror. It was called that because criticizing Adams and his government became illegal. Twenty newspaper editors and one member of Congress were jailed and many others fled the country to avoid being taken to court.

- Martin Van Buren (1782–1862) was the first president who was born an American citizen. The prior seven presidents were born British subjects.

- Thomas Jefferson (1743–1826) had a pet mockingbird named Dick that he trained to sing alongside him while he played the violin.

- James Madison (1751–1836) was the first president to wear long pants instead of short pants, or knickers.

- While he was president, John Quincy Adams (1767–1848) enjoyed skinny-dipping in the nearby Potomac River. On one occasion, someone stole his clothes and Adams had to ask a passing boy to go to the White House to fetch some more.

- William Henry Harrison (1773–1841) delivered his two-hour inaugural address on a cold winter's day. He did not wear a hat, a coat, or gloves that day and developed a case of pneumonia. A month later, he died.

- John Tyler (1790–1862), the man who succeeded William Henry Harrison, was playing a game of marbles with his sons when he was informed that he had just become president.

- Andrew Johnson (1808–1875) had never been to school when he married at age 18. His wife, Eliza, taught him to read and write.

- Ulysses S. Grant (1822–1885) was very small and shy when he was a boy. Other boys in town gave him the nickname "Useless" because he was so tiny and could not hold his own in games. The lonely boy sought companionship from horses and became an outstanding horseman.

- Rutherford B. Hayes (1822–1893) was the first president to use a telephone. His phone number was "1."

- The Baby Ruth candy bar was named after Ruth Cleveland (1891–1904), the daughter of President Grover Cleveland (1837–1908).

- Benjamin Harrison (1833–1901), the 23rd president of the United States, was the grandson of William Henry Harrison, the 9th president. Both men were also generals in the army.

- Many U.S. presidents were given nick-names by people who liked or disliked them.

George Washington	Old Fox
John Adams	His Rotundity
Andrew Jackson	Sharp Knife
Franklin Pierce	Handsome Frank
James Buchanan	Ten-Cent Jimmy
Ulysses S. Grant	Butcher from Galena
Rutherford B. Hayes	Granny Hayes
Grover Cleveland	Hangman of Buffalo
Benjamin Harrison	Human Iceberg
Theodore Roosevelt	Happy Warrior
Franklin D. Roosevelt	Sphinx

- Theodore Roosevelt (1858–1919) loved to read and usually finished two to three books a day.

- William Taft (1857–1930) was the largest president, weighing 332 pounds at his heaviest. After getting stuck in the White House bathtub, he had plumbers install a new tub that was big enough for four normal-sized people.

- Woodrow Wilson (1856–1924) kept a flock of sheep on the White House lawn.

- Franklin D. Roosevelt (1882–1945) was not only related to Theodore Roosevelt, but to ten other prior presidents.

- Harry Truman (1884–1972) did not have a middle name, just a middle initial — S.

- George Bush (1924–) was famous for disliking broccoli. Scientists say that people like Bush are justified in their distaste for the green vegetable. Some people's mouths naturally produce certain chemicals that break down broccoli into substances that taste really bad.

- When Lyndon B. Johnson (1908–1973) visited Pope Paul VI in Rome, the pope gave Johnson a valuable 14th-century painting. Johnson gave the pope a picture of himself.

- Richard Nixon (1913–1994) was an expert poker player. As a young man, he used some of his winnings at poker to help finance his first political campaign.

- Ronald Reagan (1911–) was a movie and television star before he entered politics. One of his last roles was in a 1958 TV special called *A Turkey for the President*.

- Black Farm Woman was a German peasant who led a workers' rebellion during the 16th century. She and 8,000 other pitchfork-carrying peasants marched into the villages of Weinsberg and Heilbronn, ousted the local rulers, and set up their own governments.

- Philippe Pinel (1745–1826) promoted humane treatment for the mentally ill in France. When Pinel was attacked by a mob during the French Revolution, one of the mental patients whom he had helped protected him from the mob.

- Bus driver Hamdija Osman, 36, was performing an emergency repair on a bus perched at the edge of a 400-foot cliff in the former Yugoslavia. The brakes of the bus suddenly slipped and the vehicle started rolling toward the drop. Jamming a leg under one wheel, Osman stopped the bus and saved the lives of 30 passengers.

- Maria Pepe of Hoboken, New Jersey, was 12 years old in 1972 when she became the first girl to play Little League baseball. When the Little League's head office in Pennsylvania learned that Maria was playing, it kicked every team in Hoboken out of the league. No girls allowed! The court battle that followed forced the Little League to change its rules and opened the game to all children.

- Carry Nation (1846–1911) became nationally famous in the United States for her violent hatred of liquor. The fierce, 6-foot, 175-pound woman with muscular arms was arrested many times for smashing up saloons with canes, hatchets, and rocks. To some, she was a hero; to others, a fanatic.

- Augustina Domonech was 22 years old in 1808 when the armies of Napoleon attacked the Spanish city of Zaragoza. When the stressed-out Spanish soldiers who were protecting the city decided to give up the fight, Domonech jumped into action. She took over a cannon and began firing at the French. Her heroic deed inspired the Spanish soldiers to get back to their posts and resume the battle.

- R.J. "Dad" Fairbanks (1857–1943) was called "the guardian angel of Death Valley." For more than 25 years, Dad devoted himself, without pay or reward, to saving the lives of countless people who got lost in that fiercely hot, dry desert in east-central California.

- Saint Clare of Assisi (1194–1253) was an Italian nun who founded an order of barefoot nuns. In 1958, she was made the patron saint of television. Why television? On her deathbed, Clare reportedly "saw" church services in progress even though they were taking place elsewhere.

- Claus von Stauffenberg (1907–1944) was a high official in the German army during World War II who believed that Adolf Hitler was leading Germany to defeat. Stauffenberg tried to assassinate Hitler by planting a bomb in Hitler's headquarters. The bomb went off and killed four people, but a wooden table shielded Hitler from the explosion. Stauffenberg was caught and shot by a firing squad.

- Iris Love (1933–), an American archaeologist, discovered a temple of Aphrodite, the ancient Greek goddess of love.

- Ignaz Semmelweiss (1818–1865) ran a clinic in Vienna, Austria, at a time when many women who gave birth in hospitals died of puerperal fever. Though he did not know that germs even existed, he realized that doctors were somehow transmitting the disease with their hands. He told the doctors at his clinic to wash their hands before examining any expectant women. The death rate at Semmelweiss's clinic dropped from one woman in four to one in a hundred.

- Vladimir Zworykin (1889–1982) was an inventor of television technology in the 1920s. Zworykin became bitterly disappointed that television was used to broadcast mostly entertainment shows instead of educational programs. "I would never let my children come close to this thing," he said. "It's awful."

- Hypatia (ca. 370–415) was the world's first female mathematician. She was a brilliant woman who taught at the University of Alexandria in Egypt and attracted many students. Because Hypatia was not a Christian, she was attacked and killed by a rampaging mob of Christian monks.

- In 1942, Charles Drew (1904–1950) became the head of the first American Red Cross blood bank. Drew bled to death several years later in a car accident.

- Thomas Muffet (1553–1604), an English scientist, had a special interest in spiders. He wrote the nursery rhyme "Little Miss Muffet" for his young daughter, Patience.

- The first Avon Lady was a man. In 1886, David McConnell (1858–1938), a young door-to-door salesman who lived in New York State, started Avon Calling, a company that sold cosmetics to women in the privacy of their own homes.

- Thomas Edison (1847–1931) was the first person to suggest that people say "Hello" when answering the telephone. Before that, people were advised to shout "Ahoy! Ahoy!" when answering the phone.

- Henry Cavendish (1731–1810) has been called one of history's greatest scientists. Cavendish was extremely shy and hardly spoke to anyone during his long lifetime. Because he hated being around people, he kept his many scientific discoveries a secret until his death.

- In 1951 Betty Nesmith Graham (1924–1980) was a young secretary at a bank in Dallas, Texas. Because she found herself making numerous typing errors with her new electric typewriter, she invented Liquid Paper so she could white out her typing errors and type over them. Years later, she sold her Liquid Paper business for $47 million.

- Louis Braille (1809–1852) was three years old when he accidentally blinded himself while punching holes in pieces of leather with a sharp instrument. When he grew up, Braille devised a writing system for the blind based on dots and dashes punched into paper with a sharp instrument.

- Albert Einstein (1879–1955) is considered to have been the greatest scientific mind of the 20th century. Einstein's brain was normal in size but unusual in shape. That shape may have been what enabled Einstein to bring together for the first time such ideas as space and time and to develop his revolutionary theories.

- Sir John Harington (1561–1612) made the modern toilet popular. He may have even invented it. Toilets are called johns in honor of Harington.

- Mary Anning (1799–1847) is remembered in England as the Fossil Woman. From the time she was a young girl she had a knack for finding fossils of long-dead creatures. At age 11, she and her dog found the first complete skeleton of a giant prehistoric fish called *ichthyosaurus*.

- One day in the early 1950s, the Swiss inventor George deMestral (1908–1990) came home after a walk in the countryside and found cockleburs stuck to his jacket. He examined the burrs under a microscope and saw that they were covered with hooks. DeMestral adapted nature's design and came up with the idea for Velcro.

- The guillotine was not invented by the French physician Joseph Guillotin (1738–1814). He merely advised the French government to develop a machine that could behead people quickly and painlessly. Guillotin came to regret his advice after the government used the machine named for him as a fast and easy method of slaughtering as many as 40,000 people.

• Marie Curie's (1867–1934) work killed her. The French physicist and her husband, Pierre (1859–1906), became famous and won a Nobel Prize for their research on radioactivity. Madame Curie also became the first known victim of radiation poisoning. Until then, no one knew that radiation was dangerous to human health.

- The world's first known author was Enheduana. She was a poet and priestess who lived more than 4,300 years ago in ancient Sumer (now Iraq).

I LIKE
TO READ
I LIKE TO
TALK,
I LIKE
TO WRITE
UPON
THIS ROCK.
THE END

- Cartoonist Al Hirschfeld (1903–) is famous for his caricatures of celebrities. He weaves the name of his daughter, Nina, into every caricature. At one time, bomber pilots in the U.S. Air Force were trained to find targets by doing "Nina searches" of Hirschfeld's drawings.

- Grandma Moses (1860–1961) was seventy years old before she began her illustrious painting career. She painted until almost the end of her life at age 101.

- Agatha Christie (1890–1976) is history's top-selling writer of fiction. Her 78 crime novels have sold more than two billion copies.

- Vincent van Gogh (1853–1890) sold only one painting during his lifetime and was always poor. One hundred years after his death, one of his pictures sold for $82.5 million, the highest amount ever paid for a single painting.

- Rudyard Kipling (1865–1936), the English author of *The Jungle Book* and *Captains Courageous*, lived in Vermont for five years. While he was there, he invented the game of snow golf. He painted golf balls red so that he could find them in the snow.

- Miguel de Cervantes (1547–1616), the Spanish author of *Don Quixote*, was captured by pirates and held for ransom in northern Africa for five years.

- Hans Christian Andersen (1805–1875) wrote many of the world's best-loved fairy tales, including "The Ugly Duckling" and "The Little Mermaid." Andersen was terribly afraid of death and sometimes put a sign next to his bed that said I AM NOT REALLY DEAD so that his friends would know he was just sleeping.

- Pablo Picasso (1881–1973) produced more works of art than any other painter in history. He turned out 147,800 paintings, prints, illustrations, engravings, sculptures, and ceramics. The total value of his work is $800 million.

- Aeschylus (525–456 B.C.) wrote some of the greatest Greek tragedies. He reportedly died when a flying eagle that was carrying a turtle mistook his bald head for a rock and dropped the turtle on him.

- A man named William Shakspeare (1564–1616) lived in England about four hundred years ago. However, some scholars believe that he was not the author of the plays and poems of William Shakespeare. They believe that those celebrated works were actually written by another man, Edward de Vere, the 17th Earl of Oxford (1550–1604).

- The American poet Carl Sandburg (1878–1967) was sent to jail at age 14 for skinny-dipping in a city pond.

- Louisa May Alcott (1832–1888) wrote many beloved novels for children, including *Little Women* and *Little Men*. Using a pen name, A.M. Barnard, she also wrote racy short stories about drugs and murder.

- Poet Emily Dickinson (1830–1886) spent most of her time alone in her house with her books, which were her preferred companions. Dickinson wrote more than 1,700 poems, but only a few were published while she was alive and none under her name.

- Samuel Johnson (1709–1784) was a great scholar, poet, and playwright who wrote the first dictionary of the English language. Johnson exhibited many odd behaviors that scared people away from him. Sometimes he made bizarre faces and noises for no reason and lunged at food like a wild animal.

- Harry Colebourn, a veterinarian in the Canadian army, bought a baby bear in 1914 and named it Winnipeg after Colebourn's hometown. When Colebourn was shipped overseas, he took Winnie with him and donated the bear to the London Zoo. Winnie became extremely popular there — so popular that writer A.A. Milne (1882–1956) named his fictional teddy bear, Winnie-the-Pooh, after Winnie.

- Mi Fei (1051–1107), one of China's great painters, was called Mi the Crazy One because he adored rocks. When he found a beautiful rock, he would kneel before it and call it Father-in-law. He slept with one special stone for three days.

- Painter James McNeill Whistler (1834–1903) once asked his mother to stand for a portrait. Mom got so pooped standing that she had to sit in a chair. The resulting portrait was the famous "Arrangement in Gray and Black," better known as "Whistler's Mother."

- Samuel Clemens (1835–1910) adopted the pen name Mark Twain at age 27 while working for a Nevada newspaper. The pen name comes from a term used on riverboats that means "two fathoms" (12 feet deep).

- Aphra Behn (1640–1689) was the first Englishwoman to earn a living by writing. Her life was as exciting as her plays and novels. She lived through the Great Plague, spied for King Charles II, and was thrown in jail because she couldn't pay her debts.

- Nobel-prize-winning playwright Samuel Beckett (1906–1989) wrote what some say is history's most unusual play. Called *Breath*, it lasts just 30 seconds and has no actors and no dialogue.

- Thomas "Butterfingers" Moran (1892–1971) was America's dean of pickpockets. He stole an estimated 50,000 wallets and made about $500,000 during his career. Butterfingers said picking pockets gave him a chance to travel — he was arrested in almost every state.

- The lightest known adult in history was Lucia Zarate (1863–1889). At age 17, she measured 26.5 inches tall and weighed just 4.7 pounds. She "plumped up" after that and weighed 13 pounds by age 20.

- Sara Winchester (1839–1922) thought she would die if she stopped adding rooms to her house in San Jose, California. When she finally did die, her eight-story Winchester House had 160 rooms, 10,000 windows, 2,000 doors, 47 fireplaces, and miles of secret passages and hallways.

- William Brodie (1741–1788) was a highly respected Scottish carpenter who read his Bible in public and always dressed in white. At night, however, Brodie led a gang of robbers and was eventually hanged for his crimes. His story was the inspiration for Robert Louis Stevenson's chilling novel *The Strange Case of Dr. Jekyll and Mr. Hyde*, written in 1886.

- Hetty Green (1834–1916) was one of the richest — and probably one of the stingiest — women in American history. She could afford the finest outfits, but she wore shabby, unwashed clothes. When her young son, Ned, injured himself, she refused to pay for a doctor. Instead she took him to a charity hospital. While scolding a friend's cook for using whole milk instead of less expensive skim milk, she suffered the first of a series of strokes that killed her.

• Another notorious pennypincher was Daniel Dancer, an 18th-century Englishman. The wealthy Dancer washed with sand instead of soap and used the sun instead of a towel to dry himself. Too cheap to even light a fire, Dancer would put his dinner between two metal plates and sit on it until the heat from his body warmed the food.

• Ferdinand Waldo Demara Jr. (1922–1982) was known as "The Great Imposter" during his lifetime. The 350-pound Demara successfully posed as a college dean, a doctor of psychology, a prison warden, a schoolteacher, and a surgeon.

- "Diamond Jim" Brady (1856–1917), a wealthy American businessman, had a humongous appetite. A typical dinner might find Brady pigging out on six dozen oysters, six venison chops, a couple of ducks, a saddle of lamb, a dozen-egg omelet, and six pounds of chocolates. Sitting down to a meal, Brady would leave four inches between his stomach and the table. When his stomach touched the table, he knew he had had enough to eat.

- In 1895, a young American boy named Tom drank a bowl of clam chowder so hot it destroyed his esophagus, the muscular tube between the throat and the stomach. So that Tom could get nourishment, his doctors made a permanent hole in his stomach into which his meals were poured. Doctors observed the behavior of Tom's stomach for years after that.

- "Black Bart" was a mysterious bandit who robbed stagecoaches in the American West during the 1870s and 1880s. He held up the stages wearing a white flour sack over his head and usually left behind a note of apology or a little poem. One of his ditties read:

   I've traveled many a mile
   To meet with you today
   And I leave you with a smile
   As I take your money away.

- Tom Leppard of the Isle of Skye in Scotland had his skin tattooed to look like the spotted coat of a leopard. The tattoo covers 99.2 percent of his body.

- Catherine Deshayes de Monvoisin met a fiery end when the French government had her burned to death at a public execution in 1650. Her crime? Peddling poison to hundreds of men and women who used the toxic potions to kill spouses and romantic rivals.

- Edward "Blackbeard" Teach (?–1718) was one of the most bloodthirsty pirates who ever lived. One time he cut off the ears of one of his captives and then forced the man to eat them.